DELANEY
STREET
PRESS

A Grandmother's Love Lasts a Lifetime

A Grandmother's Love
Lasts a Lifetime

By Mary Carlisle Beasley

DELANEY STREET PRESS
Nashville, TN: (800) 256-8584

ISBN 1-58334-059-9

The ideas expressed in this book are not, in all cases, exact quotations, as some have been edited for clarity and brevity. In all cases, the author has attempted to maintain the speaker's original intent. In some cases, material for this book was obtained from secondary sources, primarily print media. While every effort was made to ensure the accuracy of these sources, the accuracy cannot be guaranteed. For additions, deletions, corrections or clarifications in future editions of this text, please write DELANEY STREET PRESS.

Printed in the United States of America
1 2 3 4 5 6 7 8 9 10 • 00 01 02 03 04
Cover Design by Bart Dawson
Typesetting by Sue Gerdes

ACKNOWLEDGMENTS

The author gratefully acknowledges the helpful support of Angela Beasley Freeman, Dick and Mary Freeman, Mary Susan Freeman, Carli Freeman, Jim Gallery, and the entire team of professionals at DELANEY STREET PRESS and WALNUT GROVE PRESS.

For Virginia Criswell
and Marie Freeman

Table of Contents

A Grandmother's Love
Lasts a Lifetime

Grandmothers are very special people indeed. They care for the family and light the way for future generations by making time to share their wisdom, their hopes, their faith, and, above all, their love.

Through words and deeds, a grandmother's influence extends beyond time and space, weaving itself as an unbroken thread through future generations. In truth, a grandmother's impact upon her family lasts a lifetime...and beyond.

This little book pays tribute to grandmothers everywhere. On the pages that follow, we consider how these blessed women shape the world using a mixture of tenderness, grandmotherly advice, and enough love to last more than a lifetime.

1

A Grandmother Is...

A grandmother is many things: She is the matriarch of the family, its keeper of traditions, its historian, and its mentor. A grandmother is a spiritual guide, a role model, a trusted friend, and a beloved family treasure. The following quotations describe the woman without whom the family would not — and could not — exist: Grandmother.

Grandmother is just another name for love.

Old-Time Saying

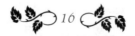

Grandparents are more patient, more tolerant, more aware of little changes in their grandchild.

Nancy Reagan

A grandparent is like a wise elder,
more detached than a parent.
Richard Walker

A grandparent is a unique kind of
emotionally involved, part-time parent
without pressure.
Dr. Fitzhugh Dodson

If a family has no grandparent,
     it has no jewel.
                    Chinese Proverb

Grandparents are the family watchdogs.
                    Lillian E. Troll

Grandparents are our living link
     to the past.
                    George Bush

Grandma was a
first-aid station who
restored us to health
by her amazing faith.

Lillian Smith

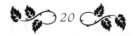

I thank God for my grandmother who stood on the word of God and lived with the spirit of courage and grace.

Maya Angelou

Her children arise up, and call her blessed.

Proverbs 31: 28

2

Love That Lasts a Lifetime…
and Beyond

Grandmothers understand the power of love, and they share that message with the entire family. A grandmother shares her love through words and — more importantly — through deeds. The beneficiaries of that love are forever blessed.

A grandmother's love becomes her permanent legacy, her timeless gift to the family. It is a gift to her children, to her grandchildren, and to subsequent generations.

The following quotations remind us of an important truth that grandmothers understand completely: Love makes the world go round… forever.

Grandparents have a special kind of love.

Eda LeShan

A grandmother is a person who has time.

Anonymous child's definition

Love is a great beautifier.

Louisa May Alcott

Whoever loves true life
will love true love.

Elizabeth Barrett Browning

He who is filled with love is filled
with God Himself.

St. Augustine

The best and most
beautiful things in the
world cannot be seen
or even touched.
They must be felt
with the heart.

Helen Keller

When you come right down to it, the secret of having it all is loving it all.

Dr. Joyce Brothers

To love is to receive
a glimpse of
heaven.

Karen Sunde

Nobody has ever measured,
   not even poets, how much
      the heart can hold.
                              Zelda Fitzgerald

Love is a multiplication.
                     Marjory Stoneman Douglas

If a thing loves, it is infinite.
                              William Blake

The story of a love
is not important —
what is important is
that one is capable
of love. It is perhaps
the only glimpse
we are permitted
of eternity.

Helen Hayes

Love is shown by deeds, not by words.
Philippine Proverb

The best portion of a good man's life
is his little, nameless, unremembered acts
of kindness and of love.
William Wordsworth

Accustom yourself continually to make
many acts of love, for they enkindle
and melt the soul.
St. Teresa of Avila

Love is not a state, it is a direction.
Simone Weil

Love is responsibility.
Martin Buber

The strongest evidence of love
is sacrifice.
Carolyn Fry

There is no love which does not
become help.
Paul Tillich

Familiar acts are beautiful through love.
Percy Bysshe Shelley

Love must be learned again and again;
there is no end to it.
Hate needs no instruction.
Katherine Anne Porter

When love and skill work together, expect a masterpiece.

John Ruskin

A woman who is loved
always has success.
Vicki Baum

Love doesn't just sit there, like
a stone; it has to be made, like bread,
remade all the time, made anew.

Ursula K. Le Guin

The giving of love is an education
in itself.

Eleanor Roosevelt

Love conquers all except poverty
and toothaches.

Mae West

Who, being loved, is poor?

Oscar Wilde

Love stretches your heart
and makes you big inside.

Margaret Walker

He who is able to love himself is able
to love others also.

Paul Tillich

Until I truly loved,
I was alone.

Caroline Norton

Love is the crowning
grace of humanity,
the holiest right
of the soul.

Petrarch

There is only one terminal dignity —
love.

Helen Hayes

Those who love deeply
never grow old; they
may die of old age,
but they die young.

Sir Arthur Wing Pinero

3

Family

A grandmother not only gives life to a family, she helps hold the family together. In doing so, she may perform a wide range of duties: nurse, chef, babysitter, counselor, and financier, to name but a few. The quotations that follow remind us of the importance of grandmothers and the families they help create.

A bonus of being a
grandmother is being
with babies and toddlers
and rediscovering
the delights of play.

Shelia Kitzinger

A happy family is but
an earlier heaven.

Sir John Bowring

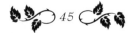

The family — that dear octopus
from whose tentacles we never quite
escape, nor, in our innermost hearts,
ever quite wish to.

Dodie Smith

Call it a clan, call it a network, call it
a tribe, call it a family. Whatever you
call it, whoever you are, you need one.

Jane Howard

A family is one of
nature's masterpieces.

George Santayana

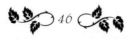

Family is the we of me.
Carson McCullers

A family is the first
and essential cell
of human society.

Pope John XXIII

No kingdom divided can stand —
neither can a household.
Christine de Pisan

Family life! The United Nations is
child's play compared to the tugs and
splits and need to understand and
to forgive in any family.
May Sarton

It takes a heap of livin' in a house
to make it home.
Edgar A. Guest

Family life is the source of the greatest human happiness.

Robert J. Gavinghurst

A large family gives beauty to a house.
Indian Proverb

A family divided against itself
will perish together.
Indian Proverb

When the whole family is together,
the soul is in place.
Russian Proverb

Cherish your human
connections: your
relationships with
friends and family.

Barbara Bush

Family jokes,
though rightly cursed
by strangers, are the
bond that keeps most
families alive.

Stella Benson

You don't choose
your family. They are
God's gift to you,
as you are to them.

Desmond Tutu

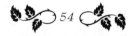

The best things you can give children,
next to good habits, are
good memories.
Sydney J. Harris

Home, in one form or another,
is the great objective of life.
Josiah Gilbert Holland

The happiest moments of my life
have been spent in the bosom
of my family.
Thomas Jefferson

Grandparents are
the living link to
the family's past.

Arthur Kornhaber

Grandmothers are full of memories.

Margaret Walker

Keep your family from
the abominable practice
of backbiting.

The Old Farmer's Almanac, 1811

4

Grandchildren Are...

A grandchild is a bundle of love wrapped in possibilities. No wonder that every grandbaby is the light of grandma's eyes. On the pages that follow, noteworthy men and women remind us that our children — and grandchildren — are our greatest treasures.

A child is the
greatest poem
ever known.

Christopher Morley

Children are our
immortality — in them
we see the stories of
our lives written in
a fairer hand.

Alfred North Whitehead

The birth of every new baby is
God's vote of confidence in
the future of man.

Imogene Fey

A baby is God's opinion that life
should go on.

Carl Sandburg

Here's my advice:
Make sure your children and
grandchildren know you love them.

Barbara Bush

Perfect love does not sometimes come until the first grandchild.

Welsh Proverb

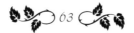

Your children are
your investment.
Your grandchildren
are your dividends.

Anonymous

Posterity is the patriotic name
for grandchildren.
Art Linkletter

When you have a grandchild,
you have two children.
Yiddish Saying

In the eyes of its grandmother,
every beetle is a gazelle.
African Proverb

Wherever children are, there is the golden age.

Novalis

5

Faith

Grandmothers, having seen it all more than once, understand the power of faith. As Grandma knows all too well, faith is the foundation upon which great lives are built. Faith is a gift we give ourselves that pays rich dividends in good times or bad.

The quotations that follow remind us of a lesson that grandmothers have been teaching since the dawn of mankind: faith protects and perfect faith protects perfectly.

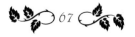

Build a little fence
of trust around today;
fill the space with
loving work, and
therein stay.

Frances Mary Buss

Faith can put a candle
      in the darkest night.
                Margaret Sangster

Seeds of faith are always within us;
  sometimes it takes a crisis to nourish
      and encourage their growth.
                Susan L. Taylor

They can conquer who believe
      they can.
             Ralph Waldo Emerson

Faith is the antiseptic of the soul.

Walt Whitman

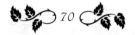

Faith is an activity.
It is something that
has to be applied.

Corrie ten Boom

Faith is the only known cure for fear.
Lena Sadler

Keep your face to the sunshine
and you cannot see the shadows.
Helen Keller

God's gifts put man's best gifts
to shame.
Elizabeth Barrett Browning

Courage is the price that life exacts
for granting peace. The soul that knows
it not knows no release from little things.
Amelia Earhart

We must have courage to be happy.
Henri Frédéric Amiel

To have courage for whatever comes
in life — everything lies in that.
Saint Teresa of Avila

Faith is a spiritual
spotlight that
illuminates
one's path.

Helen Keller

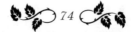

Faith sees the invisible, believes the unbelievable, and receives the impossible.
Corrie ten Boom

Faith wears everyday clothes and proves herself in life's ordinary circumstances.
Bertha Munro

Faith is like radar that sees through the fog — the reality of things at a distance that the human eye cannot see.
Corrie ten Boom

Faith is the key that fits
　　the door of hope.
Elaine Emans

Courage is fear that has
　　said its prayers.
Dorothy Bernard

The first and great commandment
　　is don't let them scare you.
Elmer Davis

Without faith, nothing is possible.
With it, nothing is impossible.
Mary McLeod Bethune

Nothing in life is to be feared.
It is only to be understood.
Marie Curie

Sad soul, take comfort nor forget,
the sunrise never failed us yet.
Celia Thaxter

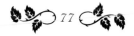

He does not believe who does not live according to his beliefs.

Thomas Fuller

Faith is the force of life.

Leo Tolstoy

To me, faith means not worrying.

John Dewey

Worry and anxiety are sand in the machinery of life; faith is the oil.

E. Stanley Jones

Faith leads us beyond ourselves.

Pope John Paul II

6

Attitude

Grandmothers understand that our thoughts have a tendency to transform themselves into reality. Grandmothers everywhere agree: A positive attitude pays powerful dividends, as the following quotations attest.

Be enthusiastic.
Every occasion is
an opportunity
to do good.

Russell Conwell

Optimism is that faith that leads to achievement. Nothing can be done without hope and confidence.

Helen Keller

There is very little difference between people, but that little difference makes a big difference: That little difference is attitude.

W. Clement Stone

One of the things I learned the hard way was that it doesn't pay to get discouraged. Keeping busy and making optimism a way of life can restore your faith in yourself.

Lucille Ball

If you think you can, you can. And if you think you can't, you're right.

Mary Kay Ash

Life reflects your own thoughts
back to you.
Napoleon Hill

The thing we fear we bring to pass.
Elbert Hubbard

Despair is an evil counselor.
Sir Walter Scott

Worry is interest paid on trouble
before it falls due.
William Ralph Inge

No pessimist ever discovered the secrets
of the stars, or sailed to an uncharted
land, or opened a new heaven
to the human spirit.
Helen Keller

It is best to act with confidence,
no matter how little right
you have to it.
Lillian Hellman

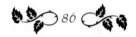

There ain't nothing from the outside
can lick any of us.
Margaret Mitchell

All human wisdom is summed up
in two words: "wait" and "hope."
Alexandre Dumas

The only security is courage.
La Rochefoucauld

The way in which we think of ourselves
has everything to do with how
our world sees us.

Arlene Raven

Human thoughts have a tendency
to turn themselves into their
physical equivalents.

Earl Nightingale

The mind is its own place and can make
a heaven of hell, or a hell of heaven.

John Milton

In the long run,
we shape our lives and
we shape ourselves.
The process never ends
until we die.

Eleanor Roosevelt

How very little can be done
under the atmosphere of fear.
Florence Nightingale

As is our confidence
so is our capacity.
William Hazlitt

A merry heart doeth good
like a medicine.
Proverbs 17:22

Act as if it were impossible to fail.

Dorthea Brande

I am an optimist. It does not seem too much use to be anything else.
Winston Churchill

It only seems as if you are doing something when you're worrying.
Lucy Maud Montgomery

A fool without fear is sometimes wiser than an angel with fear.
Nancy Astor

You must do the thing you think
you cannot do.
Eleanor Roosevelt

The fearful Unbelief is unbelief
in yourself.
Thomas Carlyle

Learning is the discovery that
something is possible.
Fritz Perls

 93

Live from miracle
to miracle.

Artur Rubinstein

7

Life

Having given the gift of life, who better to explain it than grandmothers? The following advice would make any grandmother proud. So consider these quotations and remember that life is a gift — courtesy of our mothers and grand-mothers — a gift that should be treasured and used to the fullest.

Life is what we make it.
Always has been.
Always will be.

Grandma Moses

The secret of life is
to skip having children
and go directly to
grandchildren.

Mell Lazarus

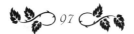

Live with no time out.
Simone de Beauvoir

Nothing is so often irretrievably
missed as a daily opportunity.
Marie von Ebner-Eschenbach

Life hurries past, too strong to stop,
too sweet to loose.
Willa Cather

If you love life,
life will love
you back.

Artur Rubinstein

Nobody's gonna live for you.
Dolly Parton

Life is my college. May I graduate well
and earn some honors!
Louisa May Alcott

Life never becomes a habit to me.
It's always a marvel.
Katherine Mansfield

What we are is God's gift to us.
What we become is our gift to God.
Eleanor Powell

Life is the raw material.
We are the artisans.
Cathy Better

Life is either a daring adventure
or nothing.
Helen Keller

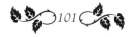

It is never too late
to be what you
might have been.

George Eliot

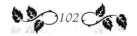

The proper function of mankind
is to live — not to exist.
Jack London

Only I can change my life.
No one can do it for me.
Carol Burnett

Give the world the best you have, and
the best will come back to you.
Madeline Bridges

It is up to each of us to contribute
something to this sad and
wonderful world.

Eve Arden

The purpose of life is a life of purpose.

Robert Byrne

All our lives, we are preparing to be
something or somebody, even if
we don't know it.

Katherine Anne Porter

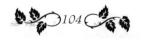

Everybody must learn
this lesson somewhere:
It costs something to be
what you are.

Shirley Abbott

When I stand before
God at the end of my
life, I would hope that
I would not have a single
bit of talent left and
could say, "I used
everything you
gave me."

Erma Bombeck

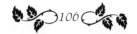

8

Grandmotherly Advice

Grandmother knows best. Arthur Kornhaber noted, "The role of teacher is one of the most important for any grandparent." And Victor Hugo observed, "If you would civilize a man, begin with his grandmother."

Such is the influence of a grandmother on future generations. With this thought in mind, we conclude with a few words of wisdom worthy of the most insightful grandma. Enjoy.

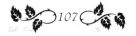

Surely the consolation
prize of old age is
finding out how
few things are worth
worrying over.

Dorothy Dix

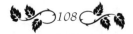

Always keep a happy attitude. Pretend that you are holding a beautiful, fragrant bouquet.

Candice M. Pope

Each day, look for a
      kernel of excitement.
Barbara Johnson

Talk happiness. The world is
    sad enough without your woes.
Ella Wheeler Wilcox

Misery is a communicable disease.
Martha Graham

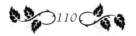

It was my mother's belief — and
mine — to resist any
negative thinking.
Audrey Meadows

An optimistic mind is a healthy mind.
Loretta Young

Life does not have to be perfect
to be wonderful.
Annette Funicello

One thing that can't abide by majority rule is a person's conscience.

Harper Lee

If you listen to your conscience, it will serve you as no other friend you'll ever know.

Loretta Young

Believe that your tender, loving
thoughts and wishes for good have
the power to help the struggling souls
of the earth rise higher.
Ella Wheeler Wilcox

Love wins when everything else
will fail.
Fanny Jackson Coppin

You will do foolish
things, but do them
with enthusiasm.

Colette

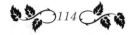

You've got to continue to grow
   or you're just like last night's
   cornbread — stale and dry.
                              Loretta Lynn

This is happiness: to be dissolved
   into something complete and great.
                              Willa Cather

God has a plan for all of us, but He
expects us to do our share of the work.
                              Minnie Pearl

Of all the things you wear, your expression is the most important.

Janet Lane

There's a beauty of age, more profound, more complete. It forms a fine patina that only life and living can impart.

Karen Westerberg Reyes

The end is nothing.
The road is all.

Willa Cather

We are all cremated equal.

Jane Ace

Sources

Sources